A to Z

COOKBOOK FOR Kids

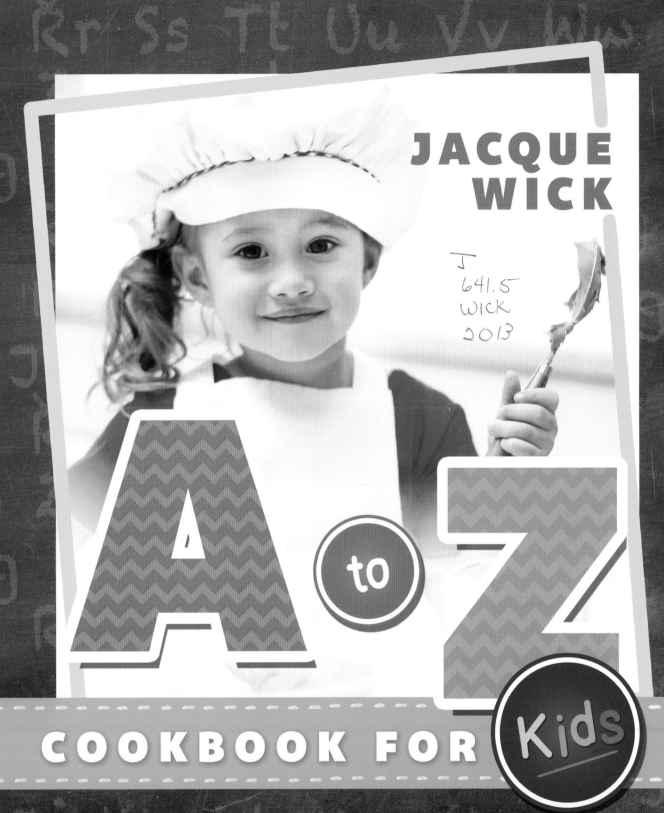

JACQUE WICK

A to Z

COOKBOOK FOR Kids

Front Table Books

An Imprint of Cedar Fort, Inc. | **Springville, Utah**

ISBN 13: 978-1-4621-1213-5

Published by Front Table Books, an imprint of Cedar Fort, Inc.
2373 W. 700 S., Springville, UT 84663
Distributed by Cedar Fort, Inc., www.cedarfort.com

LIBRARY OF CONGRESS CATALOGING-IN-PUBLICATION DATA

Wick, Jacque, 1957-
A to Z cookbook for kids / Jacque Wick.
    pages cm
  Includes index.
  ISBN 978-1-4621-1213-5
  1. Cooking--Juvenile literature. I. Title.
  TX652.5.W53 2013
  641.5--dc23
                                    2013017402

Photography by Ashley Wick Huffaker
Cover and page design by Erica Dixon
Cover design © 2013 by Lyle Mortimer
Edited by Casey J. Winters

Printed in China

10 9 8 7 6 5 4 3 2 1

would like to dedicate this book to a quote. Dedicating to a quote may seem out of the ordinary, but it feels right. Dieter F. Uchtdorf said, "The desire to create is one of the deepest yearnings of the human soul." This thought stayed with me as I worked through this book thinking of children *creating* fun recipes.

Contents

Recipes

Acknowledgments

any thanks to my photographer and daughter, Ashley Wick Huffaker. Her lifelong love of photography and people shows through the happy faces of the children.

My heart is full of gratitude for the children in the book. Although I started experimenting and finding the best recipes, the book came to life only when the children made them. Seeing them preparing the food, seeing their smiles, and then seeing their happy clapping with the final taste is a memory I'll always carry in my heart. Thanks to the parents that put up with me as I sometimes complained about hair or other details of perfection. In the end, the children were left alone to be themselves. I thank my daughter, the wise photographer, as she reminded me that they were children and that photos look best when the children look real. Of course that is the best way.

Thanks to parents and grandparents who helped to babysit the other children when their children were in the kitchen. My home became a place of friendships, old and new. Some of the children working on a recipe alone welcomed their friends or siblings in the kitchen area to prepare the food alongside them. A recipe originally planned for a single child became a photo shoot with two or more. Many thanks to all the children—they made this a wonderful experience for all involved.

Introduction

Making a way for children to create as they play in the kitchen:

Creating comes naturally to all children. How many of us remember making a mud pie in the backyard? Actually made of mud . . . hopefully never eaten. Interest in cooking comes as soon as a child can open the cabinet of pots and pans and pull every piece of cookware you own onto the floor. We all start out believing in our own ability to do everything we see our parents do. As we grow up, our confidence may be shaken. It happens to the best cooks. My feeling is that if your cake flops, fill it with Cool Whip, strawberries, instant pudding, yogurt, or other ingredients you may have in the kitchen. Even a flop can taste great. The purpose of this book is to help children learn life lessons as they gain confidence in themselves through cooking.

Advice for parents or grandparents:

The kitchen may be messier then you'd like. It's okay. Enjoy the moment. Take a photo. These days go by quickly. The kitchen will get clean, and the children do grow up. We don't want to regret the precious time we could have together as families because we are stressed about some small messes. As the child gains confidence, you can add a task or two at the end, such as letting them put away ingredients or wiping up a spill. The more difficult the recipe, the more likely a parent will need to help with the cleanup. Small children may need a sturdy stool for reaching the counter—when making the recipes in this book, the children used an ottoman, which worked great since two could be on it at the same time.

Practices for parents to share with their children:

1. Clear the area around the stove. Roll up sleeves.

2. Stay close to the kitchen when cooking on the stove or using the oven. Make sure timers are set.

3. Turn pot handles inward, toward the back of the stove.

4. Always use oven mitts when removing something hot from the oven or microwave, or if a handle is hot.

5. Make sure the stove and oven are turned off when you're finished cooking.

6. First aid: Even the best of us get a burn or cut now and then. Know what to do so you don't panic if something should happen. I would suggest children don't use the newer knives even though they cut easier. Older, duller ones are safer for new cooks.

Good cooking habits for children:

1. Tell an adult you will be cooking. Ask for help when needed.

2. Read the complete recipe before you start.

3. Gather the ingredients and kitchen tools before you start.

4. Wash your hands before you begin.

5. Most important: Enjoy yourself when you are cooking! Don't be afraid to make mistakes. The best chefs have made many mistakes, and some mistakes become a new recipe.

Making a list, checking it twice— letting children help as they learn:

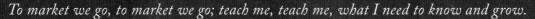

To market we go, to market we go; teach me, teach me, what I need to know and grow.

The supermarket is like a field trip for a young child. Sometimes life gets so fast we forget to slow down and use opportunities placed right in front of us. If Mom or Dad is excited about food shopping, it rubs off on the children. It's interesting to see which aisles have fruit and which have vegetables. Grocery shopping is a wonderful teaching tool that the parents are usually unaware of. If you stop and think, you can come up with many great ideas to make shopping fun and teachable.

Some things children can learn at the grocery store and in the kitchen:

1. Math: How much does the food weigh? The fruit and produce is priced by weight. Another way to learn about numbers is in the cost of food. As a teacher, I know the earlier children learn about money, the easier it is to teach them decimals and fractions later.

2. Science: Children can discover how food changes. Liquids can be frozen and then become a solid. As you heat or boil liquids such as water, you can see that it turns to vapor. The boiling liquid becomes lower in the pan as it evaporates in the air. Even how food is made can be a science lesson. Take your children to a working farm. Sometimes selective-eating children decide they like the food if they pick it from a farm. I knew one child who didn't like peaches until we went to a peach grove and picked the peaches ourselves.

3. Reading: Kids can read signs or labels. At first kids will learn simple words or the letters in the alphabet. They can see the word *Apple* or at least the letter A in the word above or below the apples in the produce aisle. You can ask them, "Where is the letter A?"

4. Writing: Your child can make a list of the food needed for a recipe. Don't worry about messy writing. If they can't write, they can draw a photo of what they need—like a picture of an apple if a recipe calls for it.

5. Imagination: Younger children can play games and activities—related to food and cooking—to build creativity and imagination. ("I'm thinking of a red fruit. What is it?")

Cooking Basics for Kids

Some ingredients are considered wet in cooking terms—like water, eggs, milk—and some will be considered dry—like salt or flour. Recipes like cookies and cake usually need both to make it cook correctly. If you added an extra egg by accident, you can add more flour to even it out; I'm not promising this always works, but most times it will. Ask a parent for help to keep from adding too much of one ingredient. And don't forget, when you're reading a recipe, "tsp." means teaspoon, "oz." means ounce, and "Tbsp." means tablespoon.

 Mixing ingredients in a bowl:

Use a large spoon to scrape ingredients from the edges so it mixes in as you also roll the mixture around and around. Grab a good spoon for mixing because it may take more strength than small hands and arms are ready for. Let a sibling hold the bowl for you.

 Cracking eggs:

Tap the egg lightly on the edge of the bowl with one hand. Put the other hand on the egg after the tap. Pull the egg apart from the broken area with your thumbs. If eggshell gets in the mix, get it out with your fingers or a spoon. Sometimes cracking eggs takes practice. You may want to crack them into a separate bowl and then pour into the recipe.

 Cutting garlic:

Garlic cloves need to be broken away from the garlic head. Lay the clove on the cutting board sideways. Cut the root off the garlic clove. Take a fork and push on the clove with the bottom of the fork to smash it. This will loosen the shell. Peel the shell off the clove. You can now cut the garlic clove into small pieces.

Cutting onions:

Start by cutting off the root. Then peel off the outside layer. Cut the onion in two pieces. Lay the onion on the cutting board with the flat side down. Cut it into slices. If a recipe calls for chopped or diced onions, cut it into smaller pieces.

is for apple

KITCHEN TOOLS:

knife

cutting board

medium mixing bowl

measuring cups
and spoons

large spoon

plate

serving bowl

INGREDIENTS:

4 oz. cream cheese

3–4 medium
Granny Smith apples

⅓ cup brown sugar

1 tsp. vanilla

1 tsp. lemon juice

After School Apple Dip

(serves 4)

1. Take cream cheese and put it on the counter to warm as you prepare the apple slices. This will soften it and make it easier to blend.

2. Cut the rinsed apples into slices on a cutting board. Cut four times like a square around the core. The core is the center of the apple. Throw away the apple core. Now you can cut the pieces into smaller slices. Be sure to turn the flat side of the apple down so it doesn't roll and slip as you are cutting. You may need an adult to help you cut the apple.

3. Put the cream cheese into a medium mixing bowl. Add brown sugar, vanilla extract, and lemon juice into bowl with the cream cheese.

4. Stir the mixture with a large spoon for two minutes. The mixture will have small lumps when it is done. Some people like it completely smooth, but I like some cream cheese as tiny lumps.

5. Pour the mixture into a smaller bowl for dipping the apple slices. You can arrange the apple slices on a plate around the bowl.

WHAT ELSE YOU CAN DO:

This apple dip is also a delicious spread for bagels or a dip for other fruit such as strawberries, cantaloupe, honeydew, or grapes.

Level of difficulty: Medium
Adult supervision for cutting

is for blending

KITCHEN TOOLS:

dull knife

blender

measuring cup

INGREDIENTS:

4 strawberries

1 cup pineapple juice

1 cup coconut water

1/3 cup sugar

1 cup ice

Blended Aloha Smoothies

(serves 4)

1. Rinse strawberries off with water. Cut off green leaves. This can be done with a dull knife. Put aside. You may need an adult to help you cut off the leaves.

2. Pour pineapple juice and coconut water into blender

3. Pour sugar into blender.

4. Put ice and strawberries into blender.

5. Mix on high for one minute. Pour into glasses to drink.

WHAT YOU CAN CHANGE:

Without strawberries, this smoothie is similar to a famous drink called a virgin piña colada.

Level of difficulty: Easy
Adult supervision for cutting and blending

is for cowboy

KITCHEN TOOLS:

barbecue grill
or campfire

aluminum foil
(12-inch x 16-inch piece)

knife

measuring spoons

tongs

oven mitt

fork

INGREDIENTS:

1 slice of orange

1 chicken thigh or small
piece of chicken

1 piece of thinly
sliced potato

1 piece of thinly
sliced onion

2 baby carrots

1 tsp. garlic salt

2 Tbsp. barbecue
sauce

Cowboy Chow Dinner

(serves 1)

1. Have an adult get a fire ready in a fire pit or warm up the grill.

2. Grab a 12 × 16 piece of aluminum foil. Pull up sides of the foil in a bowl shape to put the food in.

3. Place orange slice on bottom of foil. Put piece of chicken on top (wash hands after handling chicken). Add the potato slice on top of the chicken. Place onion slice on top of potato. Place baby carrots on each side of the chicken. Sprinkle garlic salt over the food. Pour on barbecue sauce.

4. Fold one long end of the foil over the food. Then fold the other long end. Take the shorter ends and fold them each way. Have an adult or older sibling check this so the foil is tight enough to hold the food in without leaks. Put this on the grill or in the fire.

5. Cook for 20 minutes. It will be very hot when you remove it. You must use tongs and mitt to get the cooked chow. An adult should do this for you or supervise this step. Open it carefully because it will be hot. Put it on a paper plate to eat. The foil may break through if you push a fork through it.

WHAT YOU CAN LEARN:

You can learn how to make food outside without a stove, the way early cowboys and pioneers might have eaten. You can also use a campfire. Be sure the dinner is not touching the fire but is getting heat. An adult can help you find a good spot. Some people use a campfire rack. The orange is to keep the chicken from overcooking and becoming dry.

WHAT ELSE YOU CAN DO:

This recipe can also be used with a hamburger patty. An adult can help you make a round patty from the hamburger. Wash hands.

Level of difficulty: Hard
Adult supervision for cutting and grill

is for dirt

KITCHEN TOOLS:

2 large zip-top baggies

rolling pin

2 medium mixing bowls

whisk or mixer

measuring cup

8 (8-oz.) clear
drinking glasses

INGREDIENTS:

1 package Oreo cookies

1 package graham
crackers

1 small package
chocolate pudding mix

1 small package vanilla
pudding mix

4 cups cold milk

1 (8-oz.) container
Cool Whip

½ cup pretzels broken
into pieces

1 package gummy worms

Double-Trouble Dirt Cups
(serves 8)

1. Put Oreo cookies in a zip-top baggie and put graham crackers in another baggie. Close each one tightly. Make sure most of the air is squeezed out. Put baggies on counter and crush cookies and crackers by moving a rolling pin back and forth over the bags. (You can start by smashing the cookies with hands and then using a rolling pin to make the pieces smaller.) Set the crushed cookies aside.

2. Add each package of pudding mix to two separate medium bowls. Pour two cups milk into each bowl. Whisk each for two minutes. Let them stand for 5 minutes to thicken.

3. Add half the container of Cool Whip and half of the crushed Oreo cookies to the chocolate pudding and the other half of the Cool Whip and the graham cracker mixture to the vanilla pudding. Stir each bowl separately.

4. Add 1 tablespoon of broken pretzels, a layer of vanilla pudding mixture, and a layer of chocolate pudding mixture to each drinking glass.

5. Add a layer of "dirt"—crushed Oreo cookies—as the top layer in each cup.

6. Add a gummy worm or two on top. Put dirt cups in the fridge for an hour.

WHAT IT MEANS:

The pretzels represent fossils or larger rocks underground, the vanilla mixture is like the sandy layer of ground, and the chocolate mixture is like the rich topsoil where worms like to live.

Level of difficulty: Medium

is for eggs

KITCHEN TOOLS:

oven

muffin pan

oven mitts

bowl with ice, water,
and 1 tsp. baking soda

dull knife

cutting board

zip-top baggie

measuring cup and
spoons

scissors

INGREDIENTS:

6 eggs

3 orange slices, cut in half

¼ cup mayonnaise

1 Tbsp. mustard

½ tsp. salt

1 tsp. paprika

Tasmanian Deviled Eggs

(serves 6)

Hard-Boiled Eggs

1. Set oven to 350 degrees. Put eggs in a muffin pan with each egg in separate spot. Put orange slices under eggs to keep them from touching the metal pan. This keeps the eggs from having dark spots where they touch the metal. (The dark spots will not taste burnt, so it's only for looks.)

2. Place the pan in the oven for 30 minutes. Remove pan with oven mitts.

3. Carefully put the eggs in a bowl of ice, water, and baking soda for 10 minutes. Then peel the eggs gently, starting on the larger end. Let cold water run over egg as you peel it downwards. Peel the eggs by picking a piece of shell off with the membrane and continue until it is completely peeled.

Deviled Egg Stuffing

4. Take each peeled egg and cut in half the length of the egg. Take out the yolk. Put the yolks in a plastic zip-top baggie. Add the mayonnaise and mustard. Add salt. Zip the baggie and squeeze and squeeze it until it's mixed. Push the mixture to the corner of the baggie. Make a small cut across the corner of the baggie.

5. Squeeze the mixture from baggie into the hollow of each egg.

6. Sprinkle paprika lightly over each egg. Put in the fridge until you're ready to eat.

Level of difficulty: Hard
Adult supervision for oven and cutting

is for French

KITCHEN TOOLS:

oven

cutting board
and dull knife

medium mixing bowl

fork to whisk

measuring cups and
spoons

baking pan

oven mitts

spatula

6 wooden skewers
(like a stick)

INGREDIENTS:

2 bananas

8 large or 12 small
strawberries

4 bread slices

3 eggs

½ cup powdered sugar

1/3 cup milk

1/8 tsp. cinnamon

1 tsp. vanilla

cooking spray

French Toast Skewers

(serves 6)

1. Turn on oven to 400 degrees. Cut the banana into 1-inch pieces. Wash and cut the leaves off the strawberries. Cut them in half if they are too big. Cut each piece of bread into 3 pieces; you will have 12 pieces. You may need an adult to help with the cutting.

2. Crack eggs into medium mixing bowl. Add powdered sugar and milk. Mix with fork until smooth. Add cinnamon and vanilla and mix. Spray baking pan with cooking spray.

3. Dip bread slices into the egg mixture. Turn over bread to dip on the other side. Your piece of bread should be completely covered with egg mixture. Place bread covered with mixture carefully onto the baking pan. Place in oven. Turn on timer for 5 minutes.

4. When timer goes off, check to see if toast is brown. If so, take out of oven with oven mitts. You need an adult to help you. Turn piece of toast over with a spatula. Put in oven for 5 more minutes. Then take out if the toast looks done, a light to medium brown color.

5. Cut each piece of toast into 3 pieces. You will have 36 squares. Take the banana, strawberry, and toast pieces and put them on the wooden skewers in any order. For example you can put on toast, banana, strawberry or toast, strawberry, banana.

Level of difficulty: Hard
Adult supervision for oven and cutting

Jacque Wick

is for gobble

KITCHEN TOOLS:

knife

cutting board

microwave-safe plate

microwave

paper towels

paper plates

INGREDIENTS:

Select favorite toppings:

1 large pickle

1 small onion

1 chopped tomato

1 tsp. ketchup

1 tsp. mustard

1 tsp. mayonnaise

2 hot dogs

2 hot dog buns

Gobble-Up Hot Dogs

(serves 2)

1. Chop pickle, onions, and tomato on cutting board with an adult's help. Set aside until hot dog is cooked.

2. Open package of hot dogs. You may have to carefully slit open the package with a knife. Place hot dogs on a microwave-safe plate. A paper plate will work. Put this in the microwave with a paper towel over it in case it splatters. Let them cook for 50 seconds. They will be hot when you take them out. You can place hot dog buns on a paper towel and warm in microwave for 10 seconds.

3. Put the hot dog buns on paper plates. Place the hot dogs in the buns. Add ketchup, mustard, or mayonnaise. Add the chopped ingredients you would like on your hot dogs.

4. Now gobble them up!

WHAT CAN GO WRONG:

Cutting the onion is tough. Your eyes may water if it's an onion with strong flavor. An old trick that works is to put half of a piece of bread between your lips while you cut. The bread absorbs the vapors from the onion as they rise.

WHAT YOU CAN CHANGE:

You can change the ingredients on the hot dog to warmed up chili and grated cheese to make a chili-cheese dog. The buns can be whole wheat, which may taste better.

WHAT YOU CAN LEARN:

A simple hot dog and bun can become a gourmet feast by simply adding cut-up vegetables. The American hot dog can be a fun meal since it uses most of the food groups.

Level of difficulty: Medium
Adult supervision for cutting and microwave

is for hummus

KITCHEN TOOLS:

can opener

blender or food processor

measuring cup and spoons

plate or bowl

knife (optional)

cutting board (optional)

INGREDIENTS:

2 cans chickpeas

¼ cup pizza sauce

1 tsp. oregano

2 tsp. garlic salt

1 tsp. basil

pita bread or tortilla chips

Pizzeria Hummus

(serves 2)

1. Drain the water off the chickpeas. Put chickpeas in a blender or food processor. A food processor will make the hummus smoother.

2. Add pizza sauce, oregano, garlic salt, and basil.

3. Blend for 60 seconds or until smooth.

4. Put mixture on a plate or in a bowl. Take pita bread and cut it in small triangles, or just tear it as you eat to dip in the hummus. I prefer to warm the pita bread for 20 seconds in the microwave. You can also use tortilla chips for dipping.

WHAT YOU CAN LEARN:

Hummus has been around for centuries in places like the Middle East, Africa, and Greece. The word "hummus" is Arabic and means chickpeas. Chickpeas are cooked and mashed to make hummus. There are many more flavors of hummus since it has become popular with many cultures.

WHAT ELSE YOU CAN DO:

Hummus can also be a dip for veggies.

Level of difficulty: Medium
Adult supervision for blending

is for ice cream

KITCHEN TOOLS:

ice cream spoon

butter knife

fork

plastic wrap

INGREDIENTS:

1 pint vanilla ice cream

1 premade Oreo
pie crust

1 small jar hot fudge

Cool Whip

raspberries

marshmallows

Ice Cream Dazzle Pie

(serves 6)

1. Remove the ice cream from the freezer. It may need to soften a little. Leave it on the counter for 20 minutes to thaw enough for easier scooping. Carefully unwrap the Oreo pie crust. Spoon the softened ice cream evenly into the crust until full. Smooth the top with a butter knife until even.

2. Take top off jar of fudge. Warm in microwave for 30 seconds. Pour it on top of pie. Spread it evenly.

3. Add Cool Whip on top of fudge layer of pie. Spread until even.

4. Add raspberries and marshmallows to decorate. Put pie into freezer until the ice cream has hardened.

WHAT YOU CAN CHANGE:

You can decorate the top with other small foods. Oreo cookie crumbs, mini chocolate chips, strawberries—use your imagination.

Level of difficulty: Easy

is for jammin'

KITCHEN TOOLS:

strainer

cutting board

dull knife

2 large bowls

potato masher

measuring cup

large spoon

freezer-proof jars or
plastic containers
with lids

INGREDIENTS:

about 40 large
strawberries, or two
1-pound containers

¾ cup sugar

½ (1.59-oz.) package
no-cook freezer
jam fruit pectin

Jammin' Jam

(makes 3 cups)

1. Put strawberries in strainer and rinse for 60 seconds under running water. Cut off green leaves on strawberries. You may need an adult to help you with the cutting.

2. Put strawberries in a large bowl and mash with potato masher. An adult may need to help you begin this.

3. Add sugar to a large bowl. Add mashed strawberries to sugar. Stir for 2 minutes.

4. Add pectin to the mixture. Stir for about 3 minutes.

5. Pour into jars or plastic containers. Put on lids. Keep in freezer until used.

Note: You may find different directions on different brands of fruit pectin. The directions should be for freezer jam. Have an adult look on the package. This recipe makes a lot, but you can freeze some or give some away as presents.

WHAT YOU CAN CHANGE:

You can make a bigger batch of jam. Ask for help since 80 strawberries are a lot to crush by yourself. You can use other fruit for your Jammin' Jam. The amount of fruit and sugar will be on the package of pectin that you use.

WHAT YOU CAN LEARN:

Pectin is found in plants. This substance helps the fruit and sugar bind and thicken.

Level of difficulty: Medium
Adult supervision for cutting

is for Kanga

KITCHEN TOOLS:

toaster

measuring spoon and cup

spoon

microwave-safe plate

microwave

INGREDIENTS:

1 piece pita pocket bread

2 Tbsp. pizza sauce
from a jar

5–6 pepperoni pieces

¼ cup shredded cheese
(or thin cheese slices)

other favorite toppings

Kanga's Pizza Pockets

(serves 2)

1. Tear pita bread in half. There should be a partition to tear it. Take each half and put in the toaster like you would toast regular bread. Push button on toaster like you would a piece of bread. Cook on medium. This is to dry the bread so it doesn't get mushy from the microwave step.

2. When the bread pops up, take them out carefully because they may be hot. Now you can open the middle of each piece of bread so they make a pocket.

3. With a spoon, add pizza sauce to the pockets. Smooth it around so it's evenly spread. Add the pepperoni, cheese, and other favorite toppings.

4. Put the pita pockets on a plate. Microwave them for 30 seconds to melt cheese inside.

5. Take the plate out carefully because it may be hot. Let it cool for 60 seconds before you eat.

WHAT YOU CAN LEARN:

Pita is widely used in most countries instead of sliced bread. It's a favorite of mine since I can simply put in my sandwich ingredients and eat it without the ingredients spilling out.

WHAT YOU CAN INCLUDE:

Use other ingredients you might like on your pizza: chopped onions, black olives, chopped green peppers, pineapple, ham, and barbecue chicken are some ideas.

Level of difficulty: Medium
Adult supervision for toaster and microwave

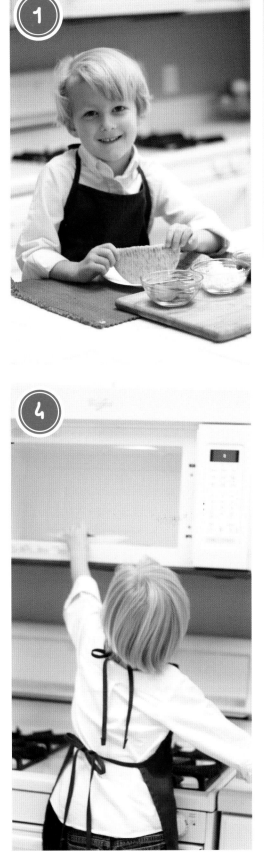

is for lemon

KITCHEN TOOLS:

knife

cutting board

juicer

measuring cups

blender

INGREDIENTS:

3 lemons

1½ cups water

⅓ cup sugar

4 raspberries

ice

Lemon Berry Aid

(serves 2)

1. Cut lemons with the help of an adult. Squeeze the juice from the lemons. You should have about ⅓ cup of lemon juice.

2. Add lemon juice, water, and sugar to blender.

3. Add raspberries to blender.

4. Blend on high for 1 minute.

5. Pour over ice and drink up.

WHAT YOU CAN CHANGE:

You can have your lemonade plain without the raspberries. Another favorite is strawberries instead of raspberries. Strawberries have a sweeter flavor than raspberries. You can experiment with both and decide which you like best.

Level of difficulty: Easy
Adult supervision for cutting and blending

M

is for marshmallow

KITCHEN TOOLS:

medium bowl

fork

measuring cups and spoons

mixing spoon

butter knife

INGREDIENTS:

1 medium banana

1 cup peanut butter

1 Tbsp. sugar or honey

1 cup mini marshmallows

6 pieces of bread

For decoration:
marshmallows, strawberries, bananas

Marshmallow Sandwiches

(serves 3)

1. Peel banana. Smash in a medium bowl with a fork. This should be about ½ cup of mashed banana. Add peanut butter, sugar or honey, and marshmallows. Stir all the ingredients with a mixing spoon for 2 minutes.

2. Take a piece of bread. Put the mixture on one slice of bread. Put another piece of bread on top. Now you have a marshmallow sandwich.

3. Decorate with marshmallows, strawberries, and bananas, and enjoy!

FUN FACT:

Half of all marshmallows sold in summer are cooked over campfires.

Level of difficulty: Easy

is for nachos

KITCHEN TOOLS:

microwave-safe plate

measuring cup

microwave

spoon

INGREDIENTS:

1½ cups tortilla chips

¾ cup shredded
Mexican-blend cheese

salsa from a jar

Buenos Nachos

(serves 2)

1. Place chips all over a large microwave-safe plate so it is covered with chips.

2. Sprinkle the shredded cheese on top of the chips evenly.

3. Put in microwave for 30 seconds to melt cheese on the chips. Take the plate out of microwave carefully. The plate may be very warm.

4. Spoon the salsa over the chips and melted cheese. Use the amount of salsa you would like.

WHAT YOU CAN CHANGE:

You can add more ingredients to your nachos. Add these before it is in the microwave: cooked shredded chicken, cooked shredded beef, refried beans. After it has been heated in the microwave, you can add chopped tomatoes, chopped black olives, chopped lettuce, sour cream, or chopped avocado.

Level of difficulty: Medium
Adult supervision for microwave

O

is for oatmeal

KITCHEN TOOLS:

oven

measuring cups and spoons

large mixing bowl

large spoon or spatula

cookie sheet

cookie scoop

oven mitt

wire rack

INGREDIENTS:

1 cup peanut butter (some brands are too watery—I like Skippy)

¾ cup sugar

1 tsp. baking soda

1 tsp. vanilla

¾ cup oatmeal

½ cup mini chocolate chips

2 eggs

cooking spray

Oatmeal Peanut Butter Cookies

(makes 45 cookies)

1. Preheat oven to 350 degrees. Add peanut butter and sugar to a large mixing bowl. Mix with large spoon or spatula until blended.

2. Add baking soda, vanilla, oatmeal, and chocolate chips.

3. Crack eggs and hold over the bowl. The inside of the eggs will fall into the bowl. You may want to practice over a different bowl and then add the eggs. Stir this mixture until blended. Set your timer for about 3 minutes stirring time.

4. Spray the cookie sheet with cooking spray. A grown-up may need to do this. Using a cookie scoop, scoop up the mixture and drop it on the pan. Put each cookie scoop about 2 inches apart. They will spread as they heat, so they need a little room. Put the cookie sheet into the oven carefully. Use an oven mitt. (A grown-up can also help you when you put the sheet in and take it out of the oven.) Set the timer for 10 minutes.

5. After the timer goes off and cookies look golden brown, use an oven mitt to take the pan out of the oven. Let an adult help you if needed. Use a spatula to put cookies on a wire rack. Wait a few minutes for them to cool, then enjoy!

WHAT YOU CAN DO DIFFERENTLY:

The peanut butter cookies can be made without the chocolate chips or without the oatmeal. If you make it without oatmeal, use a fork to make marks on the cookies before they are cooked. Wet the fork under water. Press it into each cookie.

Level of difficulty: Hard
Adult supervision for oven

P

is for popcorn

KITCHEN TOOLS:

brown paper lunch bag

microwave

oven mitt

bowl

INGREDIENTS:

4 Tbsp. unpopped
popcorn kernels

cooking spray

Possible toppings:

powdered butter, salt,
M&M's, mini Oreo
cookies, mini pretzels,
soft bite-size nuts

Popcorn Twister

(serves 1 per bag)

1. Put kernels into brown lunch bag.

2. Add 4 short sprays of cooking spray into bag. You may need someone to hold the bag open all the way.

3. Fold the top of the bag over 2 times and put into microwave for 30 seconds. Use an oven mitt to remove bag from microwave since it will be very hot. Young children need an adult to help them remove the bag.

4. Empty bag of popped popcorn into a big bowl. Add the toppings you'd like to eat with your popcorn. Maybe try something different each time.

5. You can choose to share the bowl or put some popcorn in your own bag.

WHAT ELSE YOU CAN ADD:

Raisins, dried cranberries, or mini marshmallows.

FUN FACT:

In the past, popcorn was used for decoration in addition to being a snack. The oldest popcorn was found in New Mexico.

**Level of difficulty: Easy
(after a grown-up does it with you once)**

Q

is for quesadilla

KITCHEN TOOLS:

frying pan

stove

measuring cup and spoon

spatula

plate

knife

INGREDIENTS:

cooking spray or butter

2 large flour tortillas

¼ cup shredded
Mexican-blend cheese

2 Tbsp. salsa

1 lime

Rockin' Quesadilla

(serves 2)

1. Spray frying pan with one spray of cooking spray, or put a dab of butter on pan. Turn stove burner to medium-low heat, put one tortilla in the pan, and add shredded cheese. Cover with another tortilla on top of cheese. It cooks quickly, so stay by the stove.

2. With a spatula, lift up a small part of the tortilla to see if it's browning. It will cook in about 3 minutes. Flip it over with spatula. Let it cook on the other side for 2 minutes. You can check the bottom to see if it's a light brown color. Turn off the burner.

3. Take the spatula and move the tortilla to a plate. After it is on the plate for 5 minutes to cool, you can cut it like a pizza to make it easier to share and eat. Add some salsa from a jar. Cut a lime into four pieces. Squeeze a little lime juice on for flavor. Serve with pico de gallo (see below).

PICO DE GALLO:

Stir the following ingredients together in a bowl:

3 small tomatoes, diced

½ small onion, diced

3 sprigs cilantro, chopped

juice of ½ lemon or 1 lime

½ –1 small jalapeño, chopped with adult's help (seeds removed for less spiciness)

1 tsp. garlic salt

Level of difficulty: Hard
Adult supervision for stove

is for rain

KITCHEN TOOLS:

ice trays

large mixing bowl

large spoon

measuring cups and spoons

hot drink mug

microwave

oven mitt

wooden spoon

plastic container

INGREDIENTS:

whipped cream

2 cups powdered milk

2 cups powdered sugar

1 cup powdered cocoa

2 cups powdered nondairy creamer

Rainy Day Cocoa

(serves 18)

1. Fill ice trays with whipped cream. Freeze for one hour. In a large mixing bowl, mix together powdered milk, powdered sugar, cocoa, and nondairy creamer to make Rainy Day Cocoa mix.

2. Put water in a hot drink mug until more than halfway full. Put in microwave for 1 minute and 30 seconds. Take out with an oven mitt. Younger children will need an adult to help remove the cup from the microwave.

3. Add 5 tablespoons of Rainy Day Cocoa mix to the hot water. Stir carefully so powder doesn't spill out of cup. Take out ice tray with whipped cream "marshmallows." With a spoon, remove from ice tray into a plastic container. Use some for your cocoa. Cover and return the rest to the freezer. The frozen marshmallows also cool the cocoa so it's not too hot for your tongue.

WHAT ELSE YOU CAN ADD:

Top with whipped cream. Take a chocolate bar and use the large end of a cheese grater to make shaved chocolate for a topping. Also, a candy cane is fun to add in your cocoa for the holidays.

Level of difficulty: Medium
Adult supervision for microwave

S

is for s'mores

KITCHEN TOOLS:

oven

medium mixing bowl

wooden mixing spoon

zip-top baggie

small bowl

microwave

cupcake pan

cupcake liners

measuring spoon

oven mitt

INGREDIENTS:

1 box yellow cake mix, plus ingredients listed on box

12 graham crackers, crushed

1 cube butter

Hershey's chocolate bar

mini marshmallows

S'more Cuppie Cakes

(makes 24)

1. Preheat oven to 350 degrees. Make up a batch of yellow cake mix batter, as directed on the box.

2. Smash graham crackers in a zip-top baggie (there can be some larger chunks). Put butter in a bowl and put in microwave for 20 seconds to soften butter. Mix with crushed graham-crackers.

3. Line a cupcake pan with cupcake liners. Add a tablespoon of graham cracker mixture to each cupcake liner. Add a tablespoon of cake batter to each cupcake liner.

4. Put in oven for 7 minutes. Take out of oven. Add piece of broken Hershey's chocolate on top of each cupcake. Top each with a couple of mini marshmallows

5. Return to the oven for 8 minutes. You can pull the oven door back and peek in to see how brown the marshmallows are. When they are lightly browned, the treats are done. Take them out of the oven with an oven mitt. Let them cool for 10 minutes before eating.

WHAT YOU CAN CHANGE:

For chocolate lovers, you can make this with chocolate cake mix.

Level of difficulty: Hard
Adult supervision for oven and microwave

is for toast

KITCHEN TOOLS:

toaster

plate

butter knife

small bowl

measuring spoon

INGREDIENTS:

2 pieces of bread

1 Tbsp. butter

1 Tbsp. sugar

1 Tbsp. cinnamon

Friendship Cinnamon Toast

(serves 2)

1. Place bread in toaster. Turn toaster setting to medium. Start the toaster.

2. When toast pops up, set on plate and spread with butter.

3. Sprinkle with sugar and cinnamon.

WHAT YOU CAN DO DIFFERENTLY:

Add sugar and cinnamon equally in an empty spice jar. This makes it easy to shake onto the toast for little children.

WHAT ELSE YOU CAN DO:

Try other toppings for your toast. With help from a grown-up, cut open and spoon out the inside of a ripe avocado. Mash in a bowl. Add lime juice from a small lime plus a pinch of salt. Spread on toast.

Other possible toppings: After School Apple Dip (page 8) or Jammin' Jam (page 26). Spread on toast.

Level of difficulty: Easy
Adult supervision for toaster

U

is for upsy

KITCHEN TOOLS:

medium mixing bowl

measuring cup and spoon

small bowl

wooden mixing spoon

large hot drink mug

can opener

microwave

plate

INGREDIENTS:

1 box yellow cake mix

½ cup vegetable oil

1 cup water

3 eggs

1 Tbsp. brown sugar
per mug

1 can chunky pineapple

Cool Whip

Upsy-Daisy Cake in a Mug

(Servings will vary depending on how many mugs you wish to make. May make up to 15.)

1. Pour yellow cake mix in mixing bowl. Add oil and water. (Check box of cake mix for exact measurements of oil, water, and eggs.)

2. Tap each egg one at a time on the side of a small bowl. After it breaks, hold each side of the egg and let the egg drop out into the bowl. Repeat for each egg. (If a piece of eggshell gets into the bowl, scoop it out with a spoon.) Pour eggs into cake batter. Mix with a wooden spoon for 3 minutes.

3. Put the brown sugar in the mug. Open the can of pineapple chunks with a can opener. (Some cans have a pull tab and don't need a can opener.) Add 3 pineapple chunks to mug. It's okay for some pineapple juice to get in with the pineapple. Scoop out some cake batter mix and pour it into the mug until almost halfway full.

4. Put your mug into the microwave. Turn on microwave timer to 2 minutes. Cook on high. If you look through the microwave door, you will see the cake rise above the mug. It won't fall over.

5. Take the mug out of the microwave. Normally the handle of a mug will not get hot. The rest of the mug will be hot, so only hold by the handle. Turn the mug upside down over a plate. You may need to shake the mug a little bit up and down to get the cake to fall out of the mug onto the plate.

6. Add some Cool Whip on top. Now your cake is ready to eat!

Level of difficulty: Medium
Adult supervision for microwave

**is for
van Gogh**

KITCHEN TOOLS:

paper tablecloth

new, clean paintbrushes

toaster

plates

INGREDIENTS:

assorted food coloring or
food color gels

melted butter

syrup

other decorating supplies

1 package frozen waffles

whipped cream

fruit

Van Gogh Artist Waffles

(serves 5)

1. Cover the table with a paper tablecloth in case of spills. Have the food coloring ready, the colors separated on a plate. Have brushes, melted butter, syrup, and other decorating artist supplies ready on the table.

2. Take the waffles and put them in the toaster. Put the toaster on high since the waffles are frozen.

3. Start creating your masterpieces. You can paint a house, flowers, or just lots of pretty colors. Take a photo, then eat your artist waffle. You can add syrup if you like, but it may already be sweet enough if you added whipped cream or fruit.

WHAT YOU CAN LEARN:

It's fun to mix food with art. Some chefs are great artists, showcasing their food.

**Level of difficulty: Medium
Adult supervision needed**

is for watermelon

KITCHEN TOOLS:

knife

cutting board

blender

measuring cups

INGREDIENTS:

1 seedless watermelon

1 cup yogurt

½ cup sugar

2 cups ice

Watermelon Smoothies

(serves 3)

1. Cut the watermelon in half on the cutting board. As you make your first big cut, you will need help from a parent. After it's cut down the middle, cut each of those pieces in half. There should be four pieces.

2. NOW with help from an adult, cut out the watermelon in big chunks. Then use a dull knife to cut the watermelon into smaller chunks. You should have about 1 cup of watermelon. Add watermelon to blender.

3. Add yogurt, sugar, and ice to blender.

4. Put the top on the blender. Turn the blender to medium speed. Turn it on for 1 minute. Turn off the blender. Check to make sure the drink is completely blended. If not, blend it for 1 more minute. (One minute is the same as 60 seconds. Count from 1 to 60 slowly. That will be 1 minute.)

5. Pour watermelon smoothies into glasses. This will be one of your favorite drinks on hot days.

Level of difficulty: Easy
Adult supervision for cutting and blending

is for Xtra

KITCHEN TOOLS:

measuring cups and spoons

1 medium microwave-safe mixing bowl

microwave

fork

oven mitts

strainer

INGREDIENTS:

4 cups water

4 Tbsp. butter, divided

1 box instant mac and cheese (comes with macaroni and powdered cheese)

¼ cup milk

3 Tbsp. bread crumbs or 6 crushed Ritz crackers

½ cup shredded cheese

1 tsp. dried parsley

Xtra Cheesy Mac & Cheese

(serves 5)

1. Put 4 cups water in medium bowl. Add 1 tablespoon butter, to keep macaroni from sticking together. Microwave for 7 minutes, until boiling. Add macaroni from box.

2. Cook in microwave for 5 minutes. Take out and stir with fork so macaroni is not sticking together. The macaroni should be cooked, but let an adult taste test it to see if it's done. (Some microwaves cook at different heat levels.) If it's not done, cook for 5 more minutes. Take out with oven mitts. Pour macaroni and water into a strainer to drain. After water is drained, add macaroni back into bowl.

3. Stir in 3 tablespoons butter. Then add milk and the package of powdered cheese. Stir until macaroni is cheesy.

4. Sprinkle bread crumbs or crushed crackers evenly on top of the mac and cheese. Sprinkle shredded cheese on top of crumbs, followed by parsley.

5. Put into microwave for 1½ minutes to melt cheese on top. Now it's ready to take out and eat. It will taste like oven-baked mac and cheese without using the oven!

Level of difficulty: Medium
Adult supervision for microwave

is for yogurt

KITCHEN TOOLS:

strainer

paper towel

knife

spoon

wooden spoon

measuring cup and spoons

medium mixing bowl

cutting board

serving bowl and plate

INGREDIENTS:

broccoli

celery

carrots

1 avocado

1 cup plain yogurt

½ cup mayonnaise

1 tsp. lemon juice

1 tsp. garlic salt

baked chips

Yogurt Veggie Dip

(serves 4)

1. Rinse vegetables in strainer. Let dry on paper towel.

2. Let an adult cut the avocado. There is a big seed in the middle. Once it's cut and seed is removed, you can scoop the avocado out with a spoon. Mix together avocado and yogurt in a medium bowl

3. In mixing bowl, add mayonnaise, lemon juice, and garlic salt. Mix the ingredients in the bowl until smooth.

4. Use the cutting board to cut the vegetables into bite-size pieces for dipping. You may need an adult to help you with the cutting. Put the dip in a serving bowl and vegetables on a serving plate. You can also dip baked chips.

WHAT ELSE YOU CAN DO:

Colorful potato chips are good for dipping too. They are usually made of a variety of potatoes in all colors, including sweet potatoes. We made a bread bowl for this recipe. You can buy them at a bread store, where they can even cut the top off for you. Simply scoop the bread out and you have a bowl. Another bowl could be a scooped out cantaloupe. (Cut with adult help.) Good cooks experiment with many different ideas.

Level of difficulty: Medium
Adult supervision for cutting

Z

is for zebra

KITCHEN TOOLS:

2 medium mixing bowls

2 mixing spoons

measuring cups and spoons

cupcake liners
(white, black,
or zebra stripes)

cupcake pan

oven

oven mitt

INGREDIENTS:

1 box white cake mix,
plus ingredients
listed on box

1 box chocolate cake mix,
plus ingredients
listed on box

whipped white frosting
from a can

Zebra Cupcakes

(makes 24)

1. Follow the directions for cupcake batter from the directions on the white cake mix box and the chocolate cake mix box. Make the batter in separate bowls.

2. Put cupcake liners in cupcake pan. Put 2 tablespoons of white cake batter into each cupcake liner. Then add 2 tablespoons of chocolate batter. Repeat—adding white cake batter and then chocolate batter—until the cupcake liner is over halfway full. The batter will rise, so do not fill all the way to the top.

3. Bake the cupcakes in the oven by reading the directions on the cake mix box. The cupcakes will bake into brown and white zebra stripes. Let the cupcakes cool for 30 minutes. Add the frosting carefully on top of each cupcake.

WHAT ELSE YOU CAN DO:

You can decorate the cupcake by putting a mini striped zebra cookie sideways on the cupcake. You can also buy zebra-striped edible stickers to put on top. Frosting and mini chocolate chips on top also go with the black-and-white theme.

Level of difficulty: Hard
Adult supervision for oven

Recipes by Difficulty

Easy

Medium

Hard

Conversion Chart

16 tablespoons	1 cup
12 tablespoons	¾ cup
10 tablespoons + 2 teaspoons	⅔ cup
8 tablespoons	½ cup
6 tablespoons	⅜ cup
5 tablespoons + 1 teaspoon	⅓ cup
4 tablespoons	¼ cup
2 tablespoons	⅛ cup
2 tablespoons + 2 teaspoons	⅙ cup
1 tablespoon	1/16 cup
2 cups	1 pint
2 pints	1 quart
3 teaspoons	1 tablespoon
48 teaspoons	1 cup

Index

Child Chefs
and Taste Testers

After School Apple Dip: Goldie Spilsbury

Blended Aloha Smoothies: Salote Maimoa Levatau

Cowboy Chow Dinner: Lincoln Elicio, Ayla and Braxton Burnham

Double-Trouble Dirt Cups: Max and Luke Young

Tasmanian Deviled Eggs: Cedric Fillmore, Eliza Garner

French Toast Skewers: Paisley Darner

Gobble-Up Hot Dogs: Ayla and Braxton Burnham

Pizzeria Hummus: Magdalene Rogers

Ice Cream Dazzle Pie: Lanie Blomquist

Jammin' Jam: Maimoa Levatau

Kanga's Pizza Pockets: Tyler Davis

Lemon Berry Aid: Lilly Hassell

Marshmallow Sandwiches: Magdalene Rogers

Buenos Nachos: Tyler Davis

Oatmeal Peanut Butter Cookies: Ayla and Braxton Burnham

Popcorn Twister: Cedric Fillmore, Eliza Garner

Rockin' Quesadilla: Lexie Stidham, Ayla Burnham

Rainy Day Cocoa: Paisley Darner

S'more Cuppie Cakes: Lilly Hassell

Friendship Cinnamon Toast: Magdalene Rogers, Maimoa Levatau

Upsy-Daisy Cake in a Mug: Lanie Blomquist

Van Gogh Artist Waffles: Isabelle Hawkins, Max and Luke Young

Watermelon Smoothies: Ayla Burnham

Xtra Cheesy Mac & Cheese: Isabelle Hawkins

Yogurt Veggie Dip: Goldie Spilsbury

Zebra Cupcakes: Paisley Darner

About the Author

Jacque grew up in Denver, Colorado. When she was old enough to stand at the stove, she taught herself to cook. Instantly she loved the smells and creations that came along with cooking. After college, she married the love of her life, an educator from Arizona. She then taught and worked with her husband at the family's school in Sedona, Arizona. She continued to cook as she prepared food for school parties and cookouts at their home. Tragedy struck when Jacque's husband died unexpectedly at a young age. Being a young widow with a baby and a toddler, Jacque began to publish teaching material from her home. She was a pioneer in working from home for women during that time. She has also gained experience tutoring children with ADHD. Teaching children has continued to bring Jacque happiness throughout the years. Two of her greatest gifts are her two children left to her from her husband. Recently Jacque became a grandmother. She lives in Arizona with her little dog, Kanga.

Praise for
A to Z Cookbook for Kids

"What a joy to learn to cook! And in passing, teach children to plan, perform, and complete tasks. . . . This book is a veritable ADHD curriculum guide—with good wholesome fun to boot!"

—Raun Melmed, MD, developmental pediatrician and director of the Melmed Center

"I love *A to Z Cookbook for Kids*! It has a clever layout and approach to engage the young cook's mind, with pictures that are definitely kid friendly."

—Liz Sirrine, chef and owner of award-winning restaurant Rancho de Tia Rosa

"From the grocery store to the stovetop, *A to Z Cookbook for Kids* shows how your family time can also be fun time in the kitchen while promoting imagination and teamwork."

—David M. Curran, MD, chairman of pediatric medicine, Cardon Children's Medical Center

"*A to Z Cookbook for Kids* is absolutely adorable! Jacque introduces kids to the wonderful world of cooking in an exciting way that kids can understand!"

—Jolie Vanier, youth actress and children's book author

"This cookbook is a marvelous tool for teaching important life skills and a wonderful way to create memories between parents and children that will last a lifetime."

—Chris Heimerdinger, bestselling young adult author